Two minutes a day to BITACHON

Rabbi Ben Tzion Shafier

Copyright © 2013
by Rabbi Ben Tzion Shafier & The Shmuz

All rights reserved. No part of this publication may be translated, reproduced, stored in a retrieval system or transmitted, in any form or by any means, electronic, mechanical, photocopying, re- cording or otherwise, without prior permission in writing from the publisher and author.

The Shmuz.com
866-613-TORAH (8672)
Rebbe@theShmuz.com

Typesetting by:
Shaya Sonnenschein
848-992-6597
shayason@gmail.com

Table Of Contents

1. Yankee Fans And Emunah — 5
2. What, Exactly, Is It That We're Supposed To Believe? — 8
3. The Difference Between Emunah And Bitachon — 10
4. Emunah Without Bitachon — 13
5. The Miracle Called Nature — 17
6. The World Screams Out To Its Creator — 21
7. Three Questions To Ask Your Local Atheist — 24

8. The Moment Before Creation	29
9. The Second Level Of Emunah	36
10. Hashem Knows My Thoughts	42
11. The Fourth Level Of Emunah – Hashem Is Here	47
12. Emunah And Good Luck Charms	52
13. You Can't Harm Me, You Can't Help Me	56
14. How To Take An Insult	60
15. Bashert Doesn't Mean That It Has To Be	64
16. Passing Up Your Bashert	67
17. Outcomes And Intentions	70
18. Hashem Loves You	74
19. Is Hashem Angry With Me?	78
20. Hashem Loves You More Than You Love Yourself	81
21. Stop Playing God	87
22. No Regrets	93
23. Why Is Life So Difficult?	97
24. Virtual Boxing Game	101
25. What Real Bitachon Feels Like	105

Chapter One
Yankee Fans And Emunah

When my daughter was twelve years old she was an avid Yankee fan. As the oldest child in the house, she set the tone, and it wasn't long before all of the children were Yankee enthusiasts.

One day, as we were driving past Shea Stadium, my five-year-old daughter let out a loud "boooo!" Her ten-year-old sister, sitting next to her, asked, "Why did you say that?

"That's the Mets. They stink!" Was her response.

Being a bit curious, one of the other children asked her, "Do you know what they do in that stadium?"

"No."

Do you know how to play the game?"

" No."

"Do you even know what baseball is?"

" No."

"So, why do you booo the Mets?"

"Well…everyone knows that the Yankees are great, and the Mets stink". Was her indignant response.

There is nothing wrong with a five year old having a simplistic understanding of things, and there is no harm in her being a baseball fan without knowing what that means. However, it sometimes seems that our Emunah has that level of sophistication, and our entire belief system is like a five year old's allegiance to the Yankees.

Ask the average orthodox Jew, "Have you thought about what Emunah means? Have you studied HASHEM in any significant way?

"Studied HASHEM?"

"Thought about Emunah?"

" No. Not really."

It is rather ironic that we spend so much time in the practice of our religion, yet the basics behind it, our relationship to Hashem, is something that seems to be overlooked.

Not to say that we aren't frum, and not to say that we don't believe. We do believe. We believe that Hashem is in charge. We believe that Hashem runs the world. The problem is that we don't take the time to understand what that means. If Hashem controls every activity on the planet, how does man have free will? If Hashem determines how much money I am to make, why should I go to work?

And in a real sense we are like Yankee fans. Our Emunah remains this juvenile, undeveloped sense of "I know that I am supposed to believe—I'm just not sure what exactly it is that I am supposed to believe in." Our beliefs are supposed to be much deeper, much more refined, much more sophisticated. But, for that to happen, we have to invest time and effort on understanding what we believe in. Otherwise we remain "Hashem fans".

Chapter Two
What, Exactly, Is It That We're Supposed To Believe?

There are certain catch phrases that flip off our tongues, often without our even being aware that we uttered them.

"Have *bitachon*!"

"Hashem runs the world."

"Trust in Hashem!"

They sound so nice. So religious. The question is: do we really believe them?

"It's all for the best."

"It's always good in the end. If it isn't good, then it's not the end."

What does that mean? That all I have to do is trust in Hashem, and my life will be peaches and cream, a walk in the park? Don't people suffer? What about heart attacks? Car crashes? Cancer?

"Just have *bitachon*!"

"Keep your *emunah* strong!"

So if I have *bitachon*, it will all be good? What about divorce? Bankruptcy? What about children who die? What about terrorists?

Ironically, if you ask the typical person to explain what we're supposed to believe, they can't. What does Hashem decree? What is left to man to decide? How involved is Hashem in our decisions? Where does that leave free will?

These aren't irrelevant, highfalutin questions. These are basics that all of us must deal with on a daily basis.

"Where is your *emunah* and *bitachon*?"

Fine, I'll have *emunah*. I'll have *bitachon*. But would you mind explaining to me what that means?

So, before we begin we need to define these concepts.

Chapter Three
The Difference Between Emunah And Bitachon

The Rambam defines *emunah* as the *knowledge* that HASHEM created and continues to run all of Creation.

In *Shemoneh Perakim*, he delineates the first of the Thirteen Principles of Faith: *"The Creator, blessed be He, created and orchestrates all activities, and He alone did, does and will do all actions."*

Simply put, nothing can exist and no activity can occur without HASHEM. There is no such thing as happenstance. There are no random occurrences. HASHEM is intricately involved in the running of the world.

Emunah is the understanding that HASHEM is involved in

the big picture issues. Life and death. War and famine. Disease and disaster. Which countries will go to war? Which will enjoy peace? Which economies will expand? Which will collapse?

But even more significantly, *emunah* is the knowledge that HASHEM is involved in the minutiae of my daily life. HASHEM is there with me, 24/7, 365, all day, every day, from morning to night. No human being or other power can change my destiny. HASHEM decrees the fate of man, and HASHEM is there on the scene to carry out that decree.

That is *emunah*—the clear understanding that HASHEM runs the world, from big to little, from global to local, across all platforms and situations. HASHEM is there controlling every outcome.

▶ Definition Of Bitachon

Bitachon, however, is quite different. *Bitachon* means *trust*. The *Chovos HaLevavos* defines *bitachon* as relying on HASHEM, trusting HASHEM. It is a sense of depending on Him to watch over and protect me.

HASHEM is kind, loving and merciful. HASHEM created me in order to give to me. And HASHEM wants what is for my best.

While I am responsible to be proactive, I am not in charge of the outcome, and I am not the determinant of the results. That is Hashem's role. And so, while I do my part, I rely on Hashem to care for me. *I take my heavy burden and place it on Hashem.*

Emunah is a state of *understanding*. *Bitachon* is a state of *trust*. *Emunah* comes from studying this world and seeing that there is a Creator. *Bitachon* is the state of trust that comes from recognizing that that Creator is good, kindly and wise—and that He cares deeply for His creations.

LIFE LESSON

Emunah is knowing that Hashem created and continues to run all of Creation.
Bitachon is trusting Hashem.

Chapter Four
The Difference Between Emunah And Bitachon

A person can have *emunah* and not *bitachon*. He can know that Hashem runs the world, but not necessarily trust in Him.

Pharaoh was a classic example.

The Jews were multiplying at a fantastic rate, and the Egyptians feared that they would soon be outnumbered. Pharaoh had the solution: throw the Jewish boys into the Nile as soon as they're born. The Midrash (*Shemos Rabbah* 1:18) explains that this wasn't a flippant reaction—it was highly calculated. Pharaoh said to his people, "Hashem pays back measure for measure. If we burn the babies—Hashem will burn us. If we hang them—HASHEM will hang us. HASHEM, however, promised Noach that He would never bring another flood. If we drown the babies, HASHEM will want to punish us by drowning, but He won't be able to. So we are safe."

Clearly, Pharaoh understood the power of HASHEM. He realized that HASHEM watches over the world. He also understood that HASHEM acts with justice. Pharaoh had no problem with *emunah*, but he didn't trust HASHEM—he rebelled against Him. He had *emunah*, but no *bitachon*.

▶ HASHEM Is Out To Get Me

I had a chance to see an example of this distinction in a setting closer to home. For many years I was a high school *rebbe*. One day, I was speaking to a young man about some things that were going on in his life, when he exclaimed, "HASHEM is out to get me!"

I didn't know what he meant, but then he explained. "Don't you see? It's all part of a plan. I was doing so well, and then this and this happened. Just when things were starting to get better, that guy came over and did such and such. And that sent me into another tailspin. Then, just when I was getting back into things, this and this happened. Don't you see? HASHEM *is out to get me!*"

From then on, at least once a week, he would show me how "HASHEM was out to get him."

This fellow saw HASHEM in his life. But, he didn't trust Him. Quite the opposite—HASHEM was the problem.

The point is that a person can understand that HASHEM runs the world, and still not trust Him. Even though he sees the puppeteer pulling the strings, he still may not trust the one running the show.

▶ Our Belief System

This distinction has great relevance because it is the first step in understanding *emunah* and *bitachon*. It's self-evident that if a person is to practice a belief, he must understand what it is that he is expected to believe. And so, before we try to apply concepts like trusting HASHEM, we need a clear definition of what *emunah* and *bitachon* are… and what they are not.

In the next number of chapters, we will try to further define these concepts according to the approach of the *Chovos HaLevovos*. As we explore them, we will find that there are some common mistakes—ideas and practices that many people assume are Jewish beliefs, which in fact have no connection to the Torah approach.

There is, however, a real difference between seeing a target and hitting it, so after we clearly understand the concepts, then the real work begins. For that, we need a set of exercises and growth techniques for *emunah* and a separate one for *bitachon*. Hopefully, we will map out a path for both.

Let us begin by exploring the different levels in *emunah*, which really make up the basis for *bitachon*.

LIFE LESSON

A person can have Emunah, knowing that HASHEM runs the world. And yet, not have Bitachon, because they have never learnt to trust HASHEM.

Chapter Five
The Miracle Called Nature

Imagine that I am running a Torah organization, and funds are tight. Things are so bad that it looks like we might have to close down. I decide to take action, and I'm not wasting time. I'm going straight to the top. I'm going to find myself the most famous, hidden Kabbalist in all of Israel and get a *berachah*. So I get on a plane. As soon as we land, I take a cab straight to Tzefas, and I find him—a direct descendant of Baba Sali. He's the real McCoy.

I enter the dimly lit, book-lined room where the Kabbalist is sitting. I approach and tell him why I came.

He looks right through me as he says, "I know about you. You are doing good work. I will help, but you must listen to what I say—exactly."

"Ah… yes, sir, absolutely," I respond.

"Take a plane immediately back to America. As soon as you land, go to Wal-Mart and buy sixty matchbox cars."

"Sixty cars?" I repeat.

"YOU MUST LISTEN!" he screams in a whisper.

"Yes, sir," I meekly answer.

"Then, take each of those cars and lay them out in the parking lot. There must be six feet between each car. When you are finished, go into a *beis midrash* and read from this parchment."

"Well… I… I uh…"

"LISTEN!"

"Yes, sir."

"And…" he adds as I prepare to leave, "when you have done as I have told you, wait one hour and open this letter. You will then understand."

I walk out, not quite sure what to make of what he told me,

but, hey, I have nothing to lose. So I get back on the plane, and as soon as I land, I head straight to Wal-Mart and buy those sixty toy cars. I lay them out in the parking lot, six feet between each one. I head to a nearby *beis midrash*, say the words on the parchment, and wait.

A few minutes later, I look out the window and… "Huh?!" The cars start growing. They're getting bigger and bigger. Before long the entire parking lot is filled with cars: Cadillacs, BMWs, Jaguars…

I grab the Kabbalist's letter to see what this all means, and I read: "Now, go sell those cars, and use the money well. *Chazak u'baruch*."

▶ The Miracle Of Nature

What if this actually happened? What if I watched a two-inch toy car grow into a full-sized SUV? What would my reaction be? I would probably fall on my face and say, "Miracle of miracles! This is astounding! It's beyond amazing!"

Yet, isn't this precisely what we experience every time we put a seed into the ground? From a tiny seed comes a full-size wheat stalk. From another grows a rose bush. From an acorn comes an oak tree. Is it any less astounding? Is it any less miraculous than a toy car growing into a vehicle you can drive?

Think about it. Fully edible food—exactly what need we need for our sustenance—grows out of the ground: corn, potatoes, cucumbers, tomatoes, beets, red peppers...

They aren't produced in factories. No one sits there figuring out the recipe or how long to leave them in the oven. All the farmer needs to do is plant the seed in the ground, and then that product grows from the ground, prepared and packaged, ready to eat.

What about fruit trees? Fully developed, perfectly ripe fruit, form on their own: apples, pears, oranges, grapes, cherries...

If you ever happen to walk into a cornfield at the end of the summer and the stalks are higher than your head, each one laden with many, many ears of succulent corn, ask yourself: where did this come from? A farmer planted a seed, and out came a fully formed cornstalk, with a husk protecting it, the sugars formed to ripen on time, and the meat of the corn split into bite-sized kernels. Isn't that a miracle?

Chapter Six
The World Screams Out to Its Creator

When you study nature, you see the Creator. When you look at the world around you and contemplate its many harmonious systems, all integrated, all perfectly in balance, you see Hashem.

For example…

Imagine you are seated in an ornate concert hall. The upholstery is stately, the ambiance thick. Suddenly, the house lights dim. The stage is dark. Slowly, the curtains lift, and a train of smartly dressed musicians take their places behind the eighty-one instruments arranged on the stage.

On cue, the symphony begins. First the wind instruments,

then the brass; slowly the strings join in, and then the percussion. The music is heavenly. The unity of it all, the perfect symmetry is breathtaking. Your reverie is interrupted by the fellow sitting next to you as he says, "It's amazing that they play so well without a conductor."

"What do you mean?" you respond.

"I mean, no conductor. There's no one leading them. They're just playing."

"What makes you say that?"

"Simple. I looked on stage. I don't see a conductor. So obviously, there is none."

Just because this fellow's view is blocked doesn't mean the conductor isn't there. Someone wrote the music. Someone hired the musicians. They didn't just all show up one day, randomly start playing, and there it was—Mozart's fifth concerto! The harmony, the precision, the synchrony, all demonstrate the conductor's existence.

Yet, astonishingly, people stare at the wonders of Creation and mouth the words, "I guess it just happened." A lucky roll of the cosmic dice.

And sometimes you just have to wonder: are these people serious when they say things like this? Do they really mean it?

You might even be tempted to ask them straight out, "Do you really believe that it all just happened by itself?"

Nothing in human experience just happens. Buildings don't just materialize; they require teams of architects, planners, and builders to erect them. Corporations don't just evolve; they demand coordinated teams of employees, salespeople, accounting personnel, and managers to maintain them. Computer programs don't create themselves; cadres of hundreds, sometimes thousands of people meet, discuss, plan, and then execute the coding.

Yet you expect me to believe that something so many times more sophisticated than anything that man has ever designed just randomly occurred? No wisdom, no forethought, no one guiding it? On its own, it just evolved! Kind of makes you wonder…

So, the next time you get into a conversation with your local atheist, here are three questions you can ask him.

Chapter Seven
Three Questions To Ask Your Local Atheist

Imagine you are standing in an orchard filled with orange trees in full blossom. The branches are heavy with ripe, succulent oranges stretching out as far as the eye can see. The grower explains that a mere ten years ago, it was a barren field. Over time, he planted the rows and rows of seeds, which grew into all those orange trees.

Let's think about this for a moment. Each mature orange tree began as a small white seed planted in the ground. That seed weighed a mere fraction of an ounce. But an orange tree weighs thousands of pounds.

Here is question number one to ask your local atheist: *Where did the thousands of pounds of stuff that make up the tree come from?* The roots, the trunk, the branches—thousands of pounds of matter—where did it all come from?

If you are tempted to say that it must have come from the ground, I'm afraid you'd be wrong. If you were to take a large steel vat, fill it with five hundred pounds of soil, plant an orange seed in that soil, and come back ten years later, you would find a fully formed orange tree weighing thousands of pounds, with the same five hundred pounds of soil remaining in the vat. The stuff that makes up the tree doesn't come from the ground at all.

It is created through photosynthesis. The leaves absorb the sunlight, mix in some carbon dioxide and water, and synthesize the various materials. Synthesis, of course, is the operating word. It's the process by which existing elements are manufactured into something new—something not there before. The chlorophyll in the leaves form the chemicals and compounds, and puts them together in perfect order. From thin air, it creates the bark, the wood, and the specialized plant cells needed to transfer water from the roots to the leaves. Interesting. If you owned a factory that could create stuff out of nothing, you'd be doing pretty well.

But it gets more interesting when we look at the orange itself.

When you bite into an orange, you get that sort of sweet, sort of tangy, citrusy taste. Here is question number two to ask your local atheist: *Where did the taste of the orange come from?*

Everything about the orange began from that little seed. But when you bite into that pit, it's bitter. The water that feeds the tree is tasteless. The ground that the tree grows in is also tasteless. So if the pit is bitter, and the water and ground are tasteless, where does the sweetness in the orange come from?

The answer, again, is photosynthesis. The chlorophyll in the leaves turns them into photoreceptors that capture the energy in the sunlight and create carbohydrates. These carbohydrates are then synthesized (there's that word again—creating something new) into the sugars, the tang and flavors needed to form the sweet citrus mix. Pretty impressive stuff for a leaf, no? Have you ever given an IQ test to a leaf? "Uh, excuse me, can you tell me the PH level of orange juice, and who is currently the President of the United States?"

(Please note: there are no little elves inside the tree telling it how to mix the formula. "A bit more sugar, not so much tang. Hey, go easy on the pulp there.")

But things get even more bewildering when we look at the orange itself. You see, the orange is a distinct color—

orange. And this brings us to question number three. The pit is white. The water is colorless. The ground is brown. *Where did the orange color come from?* If you dig down as far as China, you won't find orange coloring in the ground. So where did it come from?

You guessed it—photosynthesis. The leaves process some of the sucrose they create into the coloring needed for the skin. Not red—that's the color of apples. Not green—that's for pears. Not purple—that's for plums. Orange.

Now, quick: which colors combine to make orange? What percentage red? How much yellow? What is the chemical composition of pigment?

(Please note: only the outside skin of an orange is colored. That part is visible and creates the eye appeal, so color there serves a purpose. But the inside of the skin doesn't make the fruit more attractive; it would be useless to color it. And so it is white.)

Now, don't get all excited here. Don't go invoking words like astonishing, amazing, stupendous… Just remember: it's nature, plain and simple. There was a lucky role of the cosmic dice, and a hundred billion galaxies, each containing a hundred billion stars, came into being—just like that.

And each of those stars churn out unfathomable amounts of energy. Our own sun (a smallish star) transmits so much energy that despite it being over ninety million miles away, it heats our planet and warms our oceans. And even though only two billionth of a percent of its energy ever reaches here, it fuels all of life and growth on earth. And, of course, it does all this through that lucky process called photosynthesis.

And for this to function there has to be a whole host of other processes in place. The laws of organic chemistry and biophysics. The rules governing light properties and its conversion into energy. Hosts and hosts of complex systems all interwoven and all being executed flawlessly time after time, in all locations throughout the cosmos.

What a thinking person understands is that nature is the greatest indicator of the Creator, and it is the firmest proof to His existence.

Chapter Eight
The Moment Before Creation

When my daughter was six years old and we were discussing *Bereishis* (Creation), there was one issue that she couldn't come to terms with. "Abba," she said, "I understand that before Hashem created the world there was nothing, not even light and dark, but what color was it?"

The difficulty she was having is that we are so used to the world as it is that the concept of *before Creation* is hard to imagine. The idea of the absence of anything—before there was a world, before there was even matter, space, or any substance to hold it in—is difficult for us corporeal beings to fathom. We keep falling back to our way of viewing things in a physical setting, and absolute void has no place in our world.

But let's try for a moment to envision a vast empty nothingness. There is no space, no matter. There isn't even time because time only exists in a physical world. And Creation begins. Out of nothing—because there is nothing. From nowhere—because there is no place. At this absolute first moment in time, HASHEM brings forth matter, the very building blocks of creation. Then come darkness and light, not even separated, but intermingled—a patch of light here, a flash of darkness there. Next come the heavens and the earth, then the planets and the stars, the fish in the sea, the birds in the sky, and all of the animals of the earth. And on the final day, at almost the last moment of Creation, comes man.

▶ Ex Nihilo Creation

This is unlike anything in our experience—and is a point that is often missed. When man builds a house, he claims to have made something new. Yet, in reality, he *created* nothing. The wood was already in existence. The rocks were already there. Along comes man with a shovel and axe, moves things around, and claims that he *created* something new. Yet all he did was rearrange things already created.

An analogy to this would be:

▶ Frank The Cookie Baker

Every day, when Frank leaves work, he brings home two packages of freshly baked cookies for his kids. His children love to brag about the delicious cookies their father makes. Frank's kids are the envy of the entire first grade. Naturally, when the class is planning a bake sale, who do they ask for help with the recipes? Frank!

Unfortunately, Frank doesn't know that much about recipes or baking cookies. You see, Frank works in a factory. Every morning, at exactly 4:20 AM, Frank turns the switch that starts the machine, and exactly thirty-five minutes later, out roll the first batch of Stella D'oro chocolate fudge cookies.

Frank didn't create the process; he doesn't even know which ingredients go into the dough. He wouldn't be able to tell you the different preservatives and flavorings that are used. He wouldn't be able to explain the difference between radiant and convection heat, and their effect on the crispness of the cookie. He certainly isn't capable of creating the intricate system of conveyer belts, mixers, and feeder chain ovens needed to produce that cookie. His job is to flip the switch. The machine does the rest.

▶ Creative In Name, But Not In Principle

When a couple has a child, they use a system that Hashem put into place to bring forth a baby. They don't claim to be knowledgeable enough in anatomy to synthesize the proteins needed for growth. They don't allege to have sufficient understanding in physiology to weave the neuron pathways in the brain. And they certainly don't contend that they are learned enough in pathology to create the immune system that develops within their fetus.

When we use the term *made a baby*, we mean the parents used a pre-existing system that was set up with great wisdom and forethought. They pushed the button, and the gears and flywheels went into motion. Nine months later, a perfectly-formed, complex marvel called a human is born. They *had* the baby, but they didn't *create* the baby.

This is true of any creative act that a human engages in—whether it be a couple having a child, a farmer growing corn, or an entrepreneur creating an industry. We take pre-existing elements, use pre-formed systems, turn a switch—and then take the credit for the result. In our minds' eye, it is our effort that brought forth the product, but in reality, we did little but use the machinery already in place.

Hashem alone is the Creator. From nothing, He brought forth everything. And He alone conceived of, designed and formed all of it. Every element had to be thought out; there were no givens. There was no imitating or accepting the status quo—because before Creation, there was nothing to imitate or use as a model.

When we take this huge leap of understanding, we begin to recognize the wonders that are all around us, and the wisdom that is manifest throughout Creation. Most importantly, from this we gain a glimpse of Hashem. For the house itself attests to its Creator. "And if this is the Creation, what does it tell me about my Creator?"

From this perspective, nature, science, and the world itself is a source of constant inspiration. The more I understand the wisdom of the world, the more I perceive the greatness of its Creator. By focusing on this, I see Hashem with greater clarity every day.

▶ Why Aren't We Moved by This?

In actuality, we should be so moved by nature that we should have a constant stream of inspiration. We should want to sing out praise to its Creator all the time. And yet, it doesn't move us. We live with it, and it doesn't affect us.

One of the reasons is that we are so used to it. Of course, the sun rises; it has done so every day of my life. Of course, the oceans never exceed the shore; it's been that way ever since I can remember. Of course, the chicken comes out of the egg. Doesn't it always?

And so, nature, as astounding as it is, loses its impact. It loses its wow.

▶ Wow- Wonders Of The World

To help put some of the wow back into nature, we need to look at nature and its wonders with new eyes. We need to approach it as if it didn't have to be that way. If we view it from the right perspective, we will comprehend the wisdom that went into creating the world; we will appreciate the care with which everything came into being. More than anything, we will see our Creator. Not in some maybe, kind of, quasi way. We will see HASHEM—right there.

And this is the first level of *emunah*: knowing that the world has a Creator, knowing that originally there was nothing. Then Hashem said it should be, all of physicality sprang into being.

But this is only the first level of *emunah*; there are three more. Let's move on to the next.

LIFE LESSON

The First level of Emunah is knowing that, from nothing, Hashem brought forth and maintains all of creation.

Chapter Nine
The Second Level Of Emunah

On Rosh Hashanah it is written, and on Yom Kippur it is sealed: how many will pass from the earth, and how many will be born. Who will live, and who will die. Who will die at his predestined time, and who before his time. Who by water, and who by fire...

[*Tefillas* Rosh Hashanah]

The second level of *emunah* is knowing that HASHEM is involved in the big picture issues of life. Which nations will go to war and which will enjoy peace? Which totalitarian dictators will threaten world destruction? How much havoc will they be permitted to wreak? Which countries will prosper and which will suffer? Which political figures will suddenly pop up on the scene? Names that yesterday were unknown, will suddenly and menacingly take center stage. Which new technologies will be brought to the marketplace? Which cures will be discovered? Which diseases will suddenly appear? All of the issues of the coming year are reviewed, assessed and decided by HASHEM.

If you visualize the planet as a multi-dimensional chessboard, HASHEM sits as the Grand Master mapping out the moves of the coming year. This pawn will go here; this one there. This knight belongs here; the bishop over there. All of the events of the coming year are weighed, measured and determined.

In simple terms, the headlines of the New York Times are written on Rosh Hashanah. But it isn't only the headlines of the coming year that are written; every article, every feature story, and every news scoop from the global down to the local is written down as well.

The New York Times recently reported that it employs 350 full-time reporters, and hundreds of freelance contributors in fifty-three distinct news bureaus divided into local, national, and foreign territories. A single Sunday edition of the Times has more words than the entire Tanach, and reading it aloud would take over twenty hours.

Why is that? Because there are many, many issues that affect the over six-and-a-half billion people on earth. And every one of these issues is planned out by Hashem on Rosh Hashanah. Hurricanes and tsunamis, earthquakes and famine, terrorist attacks and ponzi schemes. For while Hashem gives man free will, that is only in regards to choosing. Each and every outcome remains in Hashem's hands.

Looking at the world from this viewpoint, leads to a sense of order and calm. There is a Master to the house. Anything that transpires has been weighed and measured. While I may not know all of the reasons why, there is a plan and there is a purpose. I see Hashem running the events of the world, and I no longer fear super powers and economic collapse. Al Qaeda and Ahmadinejad, Gaddafi and Hamas — they are the puppets, and Hashem is pulling the strings. And so, I read the newspapers with almost joyful anticipation—I can't wait to see what Hashem has in mind.

▶ Closer To Home

From this perspective I should feel a great sense of jubilation on Rosh Hashanah. We, the Jewish People, are servants of HASHEM, and we are also fans of HASHEM. We are His Chosen Nation, and He is our Master. During the course of the year, we suffer through the insolence and audacity of arrogant people who deny HASHEM's rule and control over the world. On Rosh Hashanah, we revel in the fact that HASHEM sits as the true Judge, meting out the fate of mankind. As such, we should feel a tremendous sense of joy, an outpouring of emotion, as we contemplate the magnificence of the *Din*.

This is the day that humanity's fate is decided. My Creator sits as the Judge. He alone determines what will transpire in the coming year. I trust in His kindness and His wisdom. And so I feel a sense of tranquility and joy. The house is in order—the Master is home.

Nevertheless, that emotion has to be tempered, because while it's grand to recognize that mankind as an entity is being judged—I, too, am a man, and I, too, am being judged. My fate for the coming year is in question. Will I live or die? Will I be healthy or sick? Will I enjoy great prosperity or not? The fate of my family, the fate of my community, the fate of my loved ones, is being decided.

▶ Understanding Life Settings

Before a man is born, HASHEM sets a life for him. He will live so many years, enjoy this level of well-being, have this amount of success. That is his life setting. Each year those issues are revisited.

Before I was put onto this planet, I may have been granted 120 years. The question is: am I now worthy of that? Based on who I am now, is that good for me? I might have been originally slated to enjoy great financial success—am I now the type of person who will use my wealth wisely, or not? The issues that are decided on Rosh Hashanah encompass the breadth of the human experience. Each person is judged, each is measured, and their fate set.

So while I should feel jubilation on this day, it needs to be tempered by a sense of awe—that my future is being decided. But both emotions should be there—great joy mixed with trepidation.

And this is the second level of *emunah*. Knowing that HASHEM determines mankind's fate. We humans seem so powerful—we aren't. We don't control the outcome. Hashem is in charge.

The first level of *emunah* is knowing that Hashem created and maintains all of physicality. The second level is knowing that Hashem is involved in the actual running of the world.

LIFE LESSON

The second level of emunah is knowing that Hashem is involved in the big picture issues of life.

Chapter Ten
Hashem Knows My Thoughts

Imagine that you hear about this Rabbi from Monsey. Rumor has it that he's a real nice man. In fact, every Friday afternoon he helps out this old widow. He shops for her. He does her laundry. He's even on his knees, scrubbing her floors. You are very impressed; he sounds like a real *tzaddik*.

But, then you find out one little detail. It seems that this poor, old widow has no living heirs—and owns an estate worth fifteen million dollars. *Oh… big tzaddik!*

Here is the point: my intentions don't color my actions—they define them. If my intentions are to help an unfortunate woman, then it is a commendable act. If my intentions are to walk off with someone's fortune, then it's deplorable. My intentions determine what the act is.

With this understanding comes a powerful recognition. If I believe in reward and punishment, then I believe that HASHEM knows my thoughts. Because if HASHEM doesn't know my thoughts, there can be no justice. It's not just *what* I did that matters—it's *why* I did it. What did it mean to me? Was my act pure or selfish? Self-centered or not?

If I believe that at the end of my days, I will be richly rewarded for what I did right, and held accountable for what I transgressed, then I accept that HASHEM knows my intentions.

▶ We Think We Know

One of the ironies of life is when we play judge and jury of others. We make all types of assumptions about other people's upbringing and background. We take it as a given that we know what's going on in their life. And then we reach value judgments, about the act and about the person. Yet, how often do we find out that we really don't have a clue?

▶ A Small Shtiebel

A number of years ago, the members of a small shul were asked not to bring little children for the Rosh Hashanah davening. It was a small building, and they wanted a higher level of decorum. As there were a number of other shuls in close proximity, they asked that anyone who wished to bring their little children to shul to daven, to please go to one of the other choices. The notices went out, signs went up and everyone knew the policy.

On Rosh Hashanah day, the *gabbai* was in shul, with his tallis over his head, absorbed in prayer. Right after *Barechu*, in walks a man with five little boys in tow. Together, they make their way across the shul, and find the row right in front of the *gabbai*. The man sits down and, one by one, the five little boys plunk down.

The *gabbai* is furious. He sent out the e-mails. He put up the signs himself. "How could he just walk in here," he screams to himself, "and sit down as if nothing's wrong!?" But it's Rosh Hashanah, it's the middle of davening, and the *gabbai* doesn't say anything.

After a few minutes, the candies start coming out. The wrappers get noisily tossed around. It's not long before one child nudges the one next to him. That one nudges him back. Back and forth. Back and forth. By now, the *gabbai* is livid. "The nerve! Some people…" he says to himself. "But still, it's Rosh Hashanah." And he does everything he can to hold his tongue.

It wasn't until a little while later, when that man and his five sons stood up to say Kaddish, that things became clear. It turns out that a woman in the community had passed away a few days ago. The man didn't see the signs, because he was sitting shivah for his wife, and his sons were sitting shivah for their mother. Then the *gabbai* was very glad that he held his tongue.

We think we know where other people are holding. We think we know what their challenges and tests are. We don't.

But if I accept that Hashem is the True Judge, then I accept that Hashem knows my intentions. Hashem knows my past; He knows me since I was born. He knows my nature and my personality. He knows what I have worked on and what I still need to work on. And, he knows exactly what this situation means to me.

As an illustration: Most school science labs have a transparent model of a man. The outside figure of the man is made of Lucite, and you can peer right into him. There are his kidneys. There is his heart, his lungs, and his pancreas.

That is an apt parable for us. When we stand in front of Hashem, we are made of Lucite. Hashem peers into the essence of us, and knows exactly what we are thinking as we think it.

This concept shouldn't be foreign to us. We end every Shemoneh Esrei with the *pasuk* (*Tehillim* 19:15): *"May the words of my lips, and the thoughts of my heart be pleasing to you."*

With those words, I acknowledge that Hashem knows my thoughts. When I daven, I don't have to speak out words for Hashem to hear them. My words are for myself. Hashem knows exactly what I want to say.

The first level of *emunah* is knowing there is a Creator. The second level is knowing that Hashem is involved in the running of the world. And this is the third level of *emunah*—knowing that Hashem reads right through me.

LIFE LESSON

The third level of emunah is knowing that Hashem knows my thoughts.

Chapter Eleven
The Fourth Level Of Emunah – HASHEM Is Here

Imagine you are walking down a dimly lit street. It's the middle of February, late at night, and you're in a part of town you don't normally frequent. You look around—not a soul to be seen. "It's mighty quiet," you think to yourself. You tighten your coat and walk a bit quicker, listening to the loud click of your heels hitting the sidewalk. Suddenly, SCREECH! A car jerks to a stop, directly in front of you. Three thugs jump out. They surround you. One of them reaches into his pocket, pulls out a gun, and points it at your head.

You've never stared down the barrel of a gun before—at least not a real one. Suddenly, you realize that your life is in the hands of this punk. Whether you live or die is in the control of this drug-crazed kid who doesn't care about you—or anything else for that matter.

Now, imagine that this little scenario has a happy ending, and somehow you make it home that evening, alive and unhurt. After the initial shock wears off, you find yourself face to face with a major philosophical problem. Since the time you've been a little kid, you've accepted that HASHEM runs the world. You even remember being taught that on Rosh Hashanah HASHEM decrees who will live and who will die.

Yet what good is that decree when your life was clearly in the hands of that punk? In fact, what good is any judgment that HASHEM sets when so many things just happen? People get sick. Drunk drivers plow into innocent pedestrians. Lone cancer cells invade healthy men.

▶ HASHEM Is On The Scene

The answer to this quandary is that if you accept that HASHEM decrees who will live and who will die, then you accept that HASHEM is there to carry out that decree. If you recognize that HASHEM determines your destiny, then you recognize that HASHEM is with you on the scene 24/7 to carry out His will.

This concept has dramatic ramifications. It means that Hashem is with you throughout your day—He's there when you get out of bed in the morning and when you close your eyes at night, when you walk down the stairs and when you get behind the wheel of your car. All day, every day, morning and night—Hashem is there, watching, guarding, and orchestrating the events of your life.

While it is true that Hashem controls the constellations, the planets, and the stars—it's far more relevant that He controls your life. Supervising, influencing, and directing all that happens. There are no happenstances, no random occurrences, no lucky rolls of the dice. Everything, everything, is directed by His will.

And, implicit in this is another major recognition. If on the previous Rosh Hashanah it was decided that your time is up, then there is nothing that you or anyone else can do to change that. It's curtain time, game over. However, if the determination was that you should enjoy another year of life, there is also nothing that anyone can do to change that. Not powerful people. Not rich people. Not influential people. And not punks carrying big guns.

Either the kid will drop the gun, or it will misfire, or some cab driver will decide to turn down that street, or the entire

NYC Fire Department will show up on a false alarm. There are many, many messengers that HASHEM uses to do His bidding. But it is HASHEM on the scene, carrying out His decree.

One of the reasons that we have such difficulties trusting in HASHEM is that HASHEM isn't "here." Perhaps HASHEM is some thirteen billion light years away, up in the heavens. But when I am walking on a cold, dark street, late at night, I am alone. It is the three of them and me. So, naturally, I am afraid. Who wouldn't be?

▶ The Ramifications Of This Are Profound

This is the fourth level of *emunah*. Knowing that HASHEM is here with me, throughout my day—when I learn, when I daven, when I eat, when I sleep. HASHEM occupies every part of the universe and wherever there is physicality, there is HASHEM.

If I fully understood this fear would be impossible. It would the equivalent to you and I walking down the street accompanied by the entire US Marine Corps, when some high school punk pulls out a switchblade and threatens us. Would it be possible to experience fear?

This concept is life changing. It affects every aspect of our existence, in ways far larger than we might realize. It brings us to a different understanding of life and our relationship with Hashem. It allows us to view situations, people and events in a vastly different manner.

This is the fourth level of Emunah, and it is the basis of our entire belief system. Because, without this, nothing we believe in makes any sense.

LIFE LESSON

The fourth level of emunah is knowing that Hashem is with me, right here, all day, every day.

Chapter Twelve
Emunah And Good Luck Charms

A generation ago, bingo games were serious fundraisers for Torah institutions. Most Yeshivas ran them, and as the staff at the game could only be volunteers, many a *yeshiva bachur* found himself "volunteering" to work the game.

Every game had its version of Sadie—an older woman in her housecoat, sitting at the end of the third row. On the table were her good luck charms—her lucky rabbit foot keychain, her lucky pennies, her winning card from last month—all laid out in exact "lucky" order. And, she sat there, waiting for her special number to be called.

"I-19."

And she would say, "I-19, that's my number!" as she held her rabbit foot even closer for better luck.

To many people, when they tell you to have *bitachon*, they mean something like this. A sort of good luck charm, a kind of wishful thinking, as in, "Have faith. Keep good cheer. Things will work out in the end." But, like Sadie, they don't really believe in this stuff, they surely don't *know* it to be so—they just *sort* of, *kind* of, *hope* that, things will work out.

And while many people "frum speak," and use the vernacular, they aren't any more sophisticated than Sadie—they just use different terms. "It's all *mazel*." "He has a good *mazel*." "Of course he does well in business; he has *mazel*." "To succeed in life, you need *mazel*."

And it could well be that when they say, "It's *bashert*," they don't know the difference between *bitachon*, or *mazel*, or Karma, or voodoo—or whatever. But it doesn't matter—because it's all the same. Just some sort of, hazy, confused, wishful thinking.

This has nothing to do with *bitachon*. *Bitachon* is based on knowing that HASHEM is active in the running of the world. *Bitachon* is founded on the knowledge that HASHEM is with me throughout my day, observing, protecting and helping me. *Bitachon* rests on the understanding that HASHEM controls every outcome. It isn't *mazel*, it isn't lucky rabbit feet—it's HASHEM.

Two Minutes To Bitachon

And before a person can reach any real level of *bitachon*, he has to have a firm grasp of the fourth level of *emunah*. He has to understand that Hashem is here—right here. Active. Involved. Present and accounted for, in the running of my life.

But there's one more point that requires understanding. Many times when people use the word *bitachon*, they mean "faith," as in, "We can't really know—but we have faith."

But faith and *bitachon* have very little to do with one another.

Faith is something that we have in people. Imagine that you offer to buy my car. You name a price, I agree, and then you ask, "Is it okay if I pay you by check?"

Hmmmm… Do I take your check or not? Well, it depends. If the amount is small, and I know you well, I probably have faith that you're good for the money. But if I'm selling my car for fifteen thousand dollars, and I don't know you that well, do I have faith that your check won't bounce?

Bitachon isn't supposed to be some sort of wistful, foggy "I hope it's true," sort of sense. It is knowledge. Knowing that Hashem is present. Knowing that Hashem is involved in my life. Knowing that Hashem will come through for me.

Once upon a time there were people who had rock solid powerful trust. The *Avos* were on that level. Avraham, Yitzchak and Yaakov walked with Hashem. Sarah, Rivkah, Rachel and

Leah spoke to Hashem. Of course they trusted. Of course they weren't afraid—how could they be? Hashem was right there with them.

For us, our work lies in making our beliefs tangible. We have to come to see Hashem. We need to train ourselves to find Him—hiding, yet controlling all. We start with the big picture issues. Looking at the world and seeing that it has a Creator. Studying the astonishing system of nature and getting a sense of awe of

the One who formed it. Then we study life on this planet. We review history—the history of the world and the history of our lives. And we discover Hashem. We see the Orchestrator behind the scenes, coordinating, choreographing all of the events of mankind's tumultuous existence. And eventually we reach that goal of seeing Hashem. Not sort of hoping, or praying, or wishing—but *knowing* that Hashem is with us.

LIFE LESSON

- **Faith is hoping that something will happen.**
- **Bitachon is knowing that Hashem will take care of me.**

Chapter Thirteen
You Can't Harm Me, You Can't Help Me

"Do not take revenge."

[*Vayikra* 19:18]

One day, you ask to borrow my shovel. I refuse. The next day, I say to you, "May I borrow your hammer?" You respond, "Yesterday, when I asked you for a shovel, you wouldn't help me. I'm going to pay you back in kind. Now that you need something, I won't help." This is revenge.

[*Yoma* 23a]

The *Sefer HaChinuch* (241) explains that the Torah forbids

us from taking revenge because everything that happens to us, good or bad, is directed by HASHEM. No one can harm us without HASHEM's will. Therefore, when someone causes us pain or suffering, we shouldn't seek to pay him back. We should recognize that that person isn't the cause of the damage. It has been directed to us by HASHEM.

The *Sefer HaChinuch* is teaching us that by taking revenge, I am denying HASHEM's involvement in my life. If HASHEM runs the world, and everything comes from Him, why should I seek to hurt this man who "harmed" me? He is but the messenger. The misfortune was directed to me by my Creator.

By seeking revenge, I impute power to man. I am acknowledging that he can hurt me. That is a misunderstanding of the way that HASHEM runs the world. I need to understand that it is HASHEM alone Who controls my fate.

▶ You Can't Harm Me

This concept is one of the foundations of *bitachon*—understanding that HASHEM decides what is best for me, and decrees what will befall me. Things don't just happen. Nothing just occurs. HASHEM decrees my fate and nothing can change that. "*No person, animal or other creation can harm me, without*

Hashem's approval" (*Chovos HaLevovos, Sha'ar HaBitachon* 3).

In simple terms, Hashem is there with me, 24/7, guiding my life, protecting me—and nothing can touch me, unless it is directed by Hashem. Stormy seas can't drown me. Hurricanes can't flood my home. Wild fires can't burn me. Drunk drivers can't kill me. Bears can't maul my children. No harm can befall me, unless it was decreed by Hashem.

On its most practical level, this means that my fate is not in the hands of man. No human being can alter my state. If I was slated to be wealthy—you can't take that from me. If I was determined to enjoy honor—you can't defame me. If I wasn't supposed to suffer—you can't cause me pain.

You may dream and scheme, but Hashem is here protecting me, guiding all outcomes. If I am to suffer, then it will happen regardless of your attempts. If it wasn't meant to, nothing you do can change that. Every ounce of pain and suffering is weighed and meted out by Hashem. No one can alter that.

▶ I Walk Around In A Bubble

A way to relate to this is to imagine that you are surrounded by a plastic bubble. When you walk down the street, you can see out of the bubble, you can hear what's going on around you, but no one can reach in. They can try to throw a rock at you, but it won't penetrate. They can try to hit you—it won't happen. They can't touch you; you are shielded by the bubble. That bubble is comparable to Hashem. Hashem is protecting you—24/7, 365, all day, every day.

And, this protection runs across the gamut of life. No one can cause you to lose a customer or a business deal. No one can cause you to be fired. No one can cause you to lose a *shidduch*. There may be people who wish for your harm, but they are powerless to change what Hashem has decreed.

This is what the *Sefer HaChinuch* is teaching us. The only reason I would seek revenge is because *you* hurt me, *you* wronged me, *you* took something from me. If I recognize that Hashem alone determines every outcome, I would never get angry. I might feel disappointment that you have chosen poorly, but anger only comes from the sense that you have *done* something to me. And that sense is illusionary. Hashem runs this world—not man.

LIFE LESSON

"No person, animal or other creation can harm me, without Hashem's approval" (Chovos HaLevovos, Sha'ar HaBitachon 3).

Chapter Fourteen
How To Take An Insult

When I was in third grade, I had a teacher who taught us how to accept a compliment. "Don't squirm," she would say. "Look the person in the eye, and say thank-you."

While this was wise advice, I don't recall any teacher telling us how to take an insult. The *Chovos HaLevavos* does (*Sha'ar Bitachon* 3): *When someone insults you causing you pain, you should turn your eyes heavenward and say, "Thank you, H*ASHEM*, for revealing a few of my many flaws."*

I am to recognize that the words said by that man, were meant for me to hear. The one who spoke was the messenger, sent by HASHEM.

Looking at life from this perspective is transformative. People shrink down to size. Hurtful words lose their sting. *I get it—it all comes from HASHEM. Obviously, I don't get angry. How could I get angry? You didn't hurt me; you didn't insult me—you are just the puppet mouthing the words. There was Someone behind the scenes pulling the strings.*

▶ Punching The Loudspeaker

Imagine that I am speaking to a large audience, and because of the size of the crowd, I am using a microphone. I go through my presentation, point by point, and then suddenly I stop. I stare directly at you sitting in the audience. Then, I turn red in the face, point my finger at you, and start yelling: "You are a good-for-nothing, lowly, worthless bum. I didn't know such foul people even exist!" And, I proceed to call you every name in the book.

How would you react? I would imagine that you would be incensed. "I can't believe he did that!" you might say to yourself. "He insulted me. He ripped me to shreds—in public, no less. What right did he have to do that?" Now imagine that you got so angry, you decided to take matters into your own hands. You stand up, walk over to the loudspeaker, and smash your fist right into the subwoofer.

That would be a foolish reaction. If you were to punch me, we could debate whether that's clever. But punching the loudspeaker doesn't make any sense. The loudspeaker didn't insult you—I did.

That is what the *Chovos HaLevavos* is teaching us. No man can harm me. If you yell at me, if you call me names, if you embarrass me—I am supposed to understand that those words are meant for me to hear. They are being directed by HASHEM right to me. You are nothing but the loudspeaker. So I am supposed to turn my eyes heavenward, acknowledge the source of the message and say, "Thank you, HASHEM, for revealing a few of my many flaws."

▶ No One Can Help You Either

But there is also a flip side—no one can help me either.

If I were destined to struggle financially, the wealthiest man in the world can't change that decree. If I was slated to be sick, my uncle could be the head of Oncology at Sloan Kettering Hospital—there's nothing that he can do for me. HASHEM metes out pain and suffering in a very measured and defined manner—and no one can interfere.

People don't make me rich. Connections don't help me get ahead. My business acumen doesn't make me wealthy. If I am supposed to get that money, it will come from this pipeline or from that one. If I'm not supposed to have that money, it may come in here, but I will eventually lose it. No one can change Hashem's decree. Across the full spectrum of the human experience, Hashem is directly and intimately involved in the running of our lives.

No man can harm me. If you yell at me, if you call me names, if you embarrass me—I am supposed to understand that those words are meant for me to hear. They are being directed by Hashem right to me. You are nothing but the loudspeaker.

LIFE LESSON

No man can harm me. If you embarrass me—those words are are being directed by Hashem to me. You are nothing but the loudspeaker.

Chapter Fifteen
Bashert Doesn't Mean That It Has to Be

Imagine it is Rosh Hashanah. I am standing in shul when suddenly a loud voice booms: "RABBI!"

"Yes…" I meekly respond.

"I HAVE BEEN SENT FROM HEAVEN TO DELIVER A MESSAGE."

"Yes, yes. Tell me. Please tell me. What is it?"

"THEY SENT ME TO TELL YOU THAT THIS YEAR, YOU WILL MAKE A MILLION DOLLARS."

"Oh my goodness! A million dollars! Wow! Wow! Thank you."

Now that I know my fate for the year, I say to myself, "This is great. I am guaranteed to make a fortune. All I have to do is sit back and wait for it to unfold. What could be better?"

So I take the year off. Why work? Why exert myself? I quit my day job. I don't even look at the newspapers. I know what's going to be. I lay back and wait for the money to come rolling in.

What do you think is going to happen?

Most likely, what's going to happen is that I am going to go hungry that year. Because when a decree is set on Rosh Hashanah, it doesn't mean that it has to happen. It means it is *available*, and I have to do my part to bring it about.

Many life situations are decided on Rosh Hashanah. Will I live or die? Will I enjoy health and well-being or not? Will I have success or not? Will I find my *bashert* this year? Will I have children? Each issue is weighed and measured, and then the decree is set. HASHEM, in His infinite wisdom, has determined what is best for me and He has made it *accessible* to me. Now I have to do my part and act in the way of nature and go and take it.

To earn a living, I have to get a job. To remain healthy, I need to eat properly and exercise. To get married, I must go out and find my *bashert*. If I put in the effort, then HASHEM will arrange that the right thing will happen—in the right way and at the right time. But if I don't put in that effort, then all bets are off. Possibly HASHEM may arrange for it to happen anyway, but more likely, it won't come about. Then, what would have been best for me and what has been set for me is lost—because I didn't do my part.

The point is that HASHEM doesn't handcuff a person to a given decree. I still have free will. And just because something was decreed, it doesn't mean that it has to come about. *Bashert* means it has been made available. And it's my job to go out and take what HASHEM has arranged for me.

LIFE LESSON

Bashert doesn't mean it has to be. It means it's made accessable and available. I still have to do my part.

Chapter Sixteen
Passing Up Your Bashert

A young man once asked the Steipler Gaon, *zt"l*, "When will I find my *bashert*?" The Steipler looked at the young man and replied, "You already passed her up when you were looking for the perfect girl."

You can pass up your *bashert*. HASHEM prepares the right person and arranges that the two of you should meet, but you still have free will. If you wake up one day and say, "Forget this whole dating thing. I'm just not getting married," most likely you won't. The fact that HASHEM prepared someone for you doesn't force you to accept her. And you can pass her by for any number of reasons.

And now we come to what may well be one of the tragedies of modern times.

▶ I Can't Find My Bashert

It seems that we are seeing more and more older singles than ever before. Good people. Frum people. Smart. Talented. Put together. And they look and look, yet they can't find the right one. They've gone out with this one and with that one. They went to this *shadchan* and to that one. This singles event and that weekend. All to no avail. They're not getting any younger—yet they just can't find the one.

And they raise their voice in an honest plea, "What does HASHEM want from me? All I want to do is settle down and raise a Jewish family. HASHEM, why won't You help me?"

▶ Why

The question is: why? Why is it that we are seeing more and more of this today? While there may not be a one-size-fits-all answer to this question, there is a perspective that is worth contemplating.

There are times when a person does everything he should,

and for various reasons, Hashem sees that this isn't the right time. But often, that's not the case. If you speak to older singles about their dating experiences, often the reason they can't find their *bashert* is obvious: they dumped him. For this reason or for that. Too much this or too much that. Not enough this or not enough that. The one thing they all have in common is, "He's just not for me. He's a good guy. He has a lot of positive qualities. But he's not what I'm looking for." And they go back to the trail, searching, ever searching, And they find themselves ten years older and not much wiser, still looking for him.

While this isn't always the case, unfortunately it isn't that rare either.

LIFE LESSON

Hashem decrees what is best, and makes it accessible—if you do what you are supposed to. But, if you don't, you can pass up your bashert.

Chapter Seventeen
Outcomes And Intentions

Imagine that Reuven walks up to Shimon, pulls out a gun and says, "I'm going to kill you!"

"No, no! Don't do it!" shouts Shimon.

Reuven responds, "You have this coming to you!" He then fires five shots, leaving Shimon dead in a puddle of blood.

If the Sanhedrin (Jewish high court) were in existence, and there was sufficient evidence, they would convict Reuven as the killer of Shimon.

Here is the question. Why can't Reuven say to the Sanhedrin, "Aren't you religious Jews? Don't you believe that

Hashem decrees who will live and who will die? If you do, then I'm not Reuven's killer—Hashem is. If it wasn't slated to happen, I could never have done it. So don't go blaming me."

Why isn't his claim valid?

The answer is that one level is claim is a hundred percent correct. If Shimon weren't slated to die, there is nothing that Reuven could have done to change that. But to allow for free will, Hashem created a system where man is held accountable for what he does.

The way it works is that if on the previous Rosh Hashanah Shimon had a decree of a year of life, then there is nothing that Reuven, or any other force in existence, could do to change that.

If, however, Shimon had a decree that this would be his last year in this world, then things get more complicated. There are times when Hashem will allow another person the "opportunity" to be the messenger. If Shimon were decreed to die that year in a violent manner, Hashem might also decree that certain individuals have the *option* of being the one to end his life. In that case, Reuven might be granted the opportunity to kill Shimon. If Reuven doesn't take that option, then Shimon will be hit by a drunk driver, a falling telephone poll, a stray bullet, or any number of other sudden, death-causing events.

But if Reuven does take this option, then he is called the

"killer" of Shimon—even though it's true that this decree was decided by HASHEM long ago and Shimon would have died anyway. To allow for free will, HASHEM gives man certain options—and if they take those options, the act is attributed to them. For all intents and purposes, he is considered the one who did the act—certainly in terms of all of man's dealings.

The underlying concept is that man is in charge of his *intentions*; HASHEM is in charge of the *outcome*. HASHEM gives the illusion that one man can change the destiny of another. If man opts on that illusion, then the act is attributed to him—even though the same consequence would have occurred without him.

▶ My Relationship To You

This perspective changes my relationships with other people in a rather dramatic form. If you try to help me, I am appreciative—for your intentions. You tried to help. That part—the attempt—is in your hands. If you tried to lighten my load, for that I am thankful. But the result, whether you succeed or not, is not in your hands.

If someone saves my life, I have to thank him for his good intentions. I have to recognize that he desired to help me, and for that I have to be appreciative. At the same time, I recognize that he was but fulfilling Hashem's decree. If he would not have been there, a speed boat would have pulled up, a log would have floated by, or any other kind of messenger would have suddenly appeared to save me. While my rescuer is credited as being the one who saved me and I have to be appreciative of his good intentions, I also have to recognize that that same result would have happened without him as well. The one who saved me wasn't him—it was Hashem.

If I needed money and someone gave me a large sum, I have to be thankful for his good wishes and his desire to help me. But I have to be mindful that if not for him, that money would have come to me through other means.

If you attempt to harm me, this concept tempers my attitude as well. I didn't ask you to be the nudnik to bring this about, but I understand that it would have happened, with or without you. So my anger at you is greatly diminished. For wishing my harm, I have my issues with you. But for bringing it about, not at all. The results have nothing to do with you.

LIFE LESSON

Man controls intentions; Hashem controls outcomes.

Chapter Eighteen
Hashem Loves You

I was speaking in an out-of-town community on the topic of the four levels of *emunah*. I spent some time dwelling on the third level: that HASHEM knows our thoughts. I explained the parable of the transparent man, and that HASHEM peers into my essence and knows exactly what I'm thinking as I think it. When I was finished, a number of people came up to ask questions. I also noticed two young women, who were hovering on the side waiting. When everyone else left, they came over to me, and one said in a very agitated voice: "This is terrible! How can I live with this?"

"What do you mean?" I asked.

"I mean this idea that HASHEM knows my inner thoughts. I feel so exposed. How can I live with that knowledge?"

Her friend explained that she was a *ba'alas teshuvah,* and she had been brought up by an abusive father. The idea that someone knows her inner thoughts was very threatening to her.

I tried to gently explain that she was being anthropomorphic—projecting human characteristics onto non-human objects. She was comparing HASHEM to people in her life. And you can't compare HASHEM to men or women or anyone. HASHEM is miles and miles above any human limitation.

"Naturally," I said, "if you view HASHEM as you do a human, then there are many things that you will find troubling. But that's the point—HASHEM isn't human. HASHEM is limitless and boundless, contained neither by space nor by time. HASHEM is all knowing and all-powerful. For us to even discuss HASHEM in any meaningful way, requires us to break out of our limited experiences.

"One of the reasons that we find it so difficult to relate to HASHEM is because His very essence contradicts all that we experience. In our world, everything is limited; everything has a beginning and an end. Trees are a hundred feet tall. Bulls weigh two thousand pounds. A dog lives for ten years. Everything we know can be weighed and measured because they are contained by limitations—they are so wide, so heavy and so tall. But HASHEM has no limitations. So, by definition, for us to comprehend HASHEM on any level, we need to step outside of our frame of reference."

While I could see that she understood where I was headed, she was still troubled. So I said to her, "I would like to ask you a question."

▶ What Did You Do To Be Worthy Of Being Created?

"Before you were created," I said, "what did you do to be worthy of being created?

"Meaning, at some point you didn't exist. Then HASHEM decided to create you. The question is, before you were created, what did you do that HASHEM said, 'Such an individual is worthy for Me to create.'

"The answer is—nothing. Because before you were created, you didn't exist. You couldn't do anything to be worthy to be created because you weren't.

"And while this may sound obvious, it is really profound. The *Chovos HaLevavos* explains that Hashem created you for one reason—to give to you. Hashem is magnanimous, loving and kind. Hashem wants to share of His good. Hashem made you—not because you were worthy, not because of anything that you did, nor because of anything that you will do. Hashem made you for one reason: to give to you.

"And there is nothing that Hashem needs in return. Hashem lacks nothing—so there is nothing that you could ever do for Him. The sole reason that Hashem made you was to share of His good with you.

"The very first point that you need to understand in your connection with Hashem is that it's a one-way relationship—Hashem is the giver and you are the receiver."

Chapter Nineteen
Is Hashem Angry With Me?

"The second question is," I said, "what could you do to make Hashem angry?

"Let's say that you decided, 'That's it. I'm fed up with Hashem, and I'm going to do something to get Him angry.' What could you do to make Hashem really mad?

"The answer is nothing. Because, quite frankly, you're not important enough to make Hashem angry.

"Hashem is the Creator of all. Hashem said, 'It should be,' and everything—energy, matter, quarks, atoms, and molecules—came into being. Hashem is also the Maintainer of physicality. Nothing can exist without Him constantly infusing energy into it.

"If Hashem ever got angry, He wouldn't need to zap a person. He wouldn't need to bring about a nuclear holocaust. Hashem would simply stop imparting energy into that person and he would cease to be. So Hashem doesn't need to get angry.

▸ Hashem Can't Get Angry

But more accurately, Hashem can't get angry. By definition, anything physical is confined. Because we are corporeal, we exist for a given amount of time. We take up a given amount of space. We can run just so fast; walk just so far. Hashem is beyond all boundaries, and beyond all confines. Hashem is in all places at all times, existing before and after time. Hashem is so above all of nature, that there is nothing that is beyond His powers and nothing that He can't do.

The reason I get angry is because I'm frustrated by my lack of power and control. But nothing is beyond Hashem; nothing is out of His control. Therefore, anger doesn't apply to Hashem.

When Hashem gives free will to man, He gives us the ability to make choices—but He governs the outcome. We control our intentions; Hashem controls the results. If man chooses evil, there are times when Hashem will allow those actions to come to fruition. And there are times when He will not. That is up to His ultimate wisdom. Either way, man has chosen to do evil, and man has damaged himself. Hashem is the Master of the Universe, and will either let that action come to bear, or He will prevent it. But at no point, is Hashem not in control. So, the concept of Hashem being angry is philosophically impossible. Hashem can't get angry.

Hashem only wants what's good for His creations, and therefore, so to speak, He could be saddened or disappointed. But the notion of Hashem being angry stems from a lack of comprehending His greatness.

To gain a mature appreciation of our Creator, we need to understand that just as Hashem doesn't need us and doesn't gain from us, Hashem doesn't get angry with us."

Chapter Twenty
HASHEM Loves You More Than You Love Yourself

The *Chovos HaLevavos* explains that in order to have *bitachon*, you must realize that HASHEM cares about you in a very real way. You must appreciate that HASHEM is deeply concerned for your good. And you must know that HASHEM loves you.

But HASHEM doesn't care about you as a mortal cares about you. HASHEM cares about you more than any person could care about you. HASHEM cares about you vastly more than even *you* care about yourself. Moreover, HASHEM looks out for your best interests. But, HASHEM doesn't look out for your interests as a friend or a loved one might. HASHEM looks out for your wellbeing immeasurably more than you or anyone else ever could. And most significantly, Hashem loves you—but not as a person loves another person. Hashem loves you more than anyone could ever love you. *Hashem loves you infinitely more than you love yourself.*

But this greatly understates the concept. When we say that Hashem loves us more than any other person does, we are still thinking of Hashem in human terms. This is so limiting to Hashem that it is in the category of insulting.

To put this into the proper light, *Chazal* use a parable. Imagine that long ago, two peasants were discussing the wealth of the king. "Why, the king is so wealthy," said the first peasant, "that he probably has a hundred silver coins."

"What?!" counters the second peasant. "A hundred silver coins? Why, I bet the king is so rich that he has more than a hundred *gold* coins!"

Both simpletons are insulting to the king. The king's wealth isn't measured in numbers of silver or gold coins. The king's treasure houses are filled with diamonds and pearls, precious metals and rubies; he owns vaults and vaults of gold and silver bars. Because the peasants are so small in their thinking, their attempt to praise the king is actually an insult to him.

In the same vein, any attempt to paint Hashem's concern for His creations in human terms is myopic. Physical beings have limits—Hashem doesn't. If Hashem cares about someone, it is limitless—without borders and confines. And if Hashem loves someone, that love breaks all boundaries and parameters.

If you were to take the most giving, loving individual you have ever known, and multiply that love by ten thousand, ten thousand times, you wouldn't even begin to understand the love that Hashem has for any of His Creations.

This is the foundation of *bitachon*. Knowing that Hashem loves you, and that Hashem looks out for your good. Without it, trusting in Hashem is foolish. How can I rely on Hashem if He doesn't care about me? How can I trust in Hashem if I am of no importance to Him? The only way that a person can develop a sense of confidence in his Creator, is by understanding that Hashem loves him to an extent that is beyond human comprehension.

If we understood the extent of Hashem's love for us, we would feel a tremendous sense of trust and reliance on Him. If Hashem is that concerned for my good, then of course I can trust that He will do everything possible to help me.

▶ Growing In Bitachon

The problem, however, is that these concepts are hard to feel. It is hard for us to imagine the unlimited; it is difficult for us to visualize something without bounds. It is too distant from our reality. Therefore, to help us grow in *bitachon* it is wise to use examples from our frame of reference.

▶ Abba, Please Make Them Stop!

When my son was five years old, he was running a high fever and complaining that his leg was hurting. I took him to the pediatrician, who examined him and ordered blood tests and an X-ray. It turned out that the little guy was running a 105 degree fever, and had a broken leg. Not good signs. The doctor feared the worst, and he immediately sent us to the emergency room. We had to find out what was going on.

At the hospital, they put him through more exams and more blood tests, but still nothing was conclusive. The attending physician told me that the only way he could rule out a life-threatening disease was to draw a blood sample from a vein deep in the thigh. I agreed to the procedure, and he asked us to wait in one of the emergency operating rooms.

By this time, it was already late at night and my son was

very tired. When the two tall technicians, wearing gowns and masks, walked in to draw blood, I don't think he was quite ready for them. But it got worse. One of these "masked men" asked me to help hold the patient down. When we had him firmly in position, the other technician pulled out a LOOOOONG needle, which he directed toward the inside of my son's thigh.

At that point, my son looked up at me, and with terror in his voice pleaded, "Abba, make them stop! Please! Make them stop!"

My heart melted. What could I say? We had to do this. So I steeled myself and looked the other way.

Baruch HASHEM, the results of the blood test were negative, and we went home with a diagnosis of a broken leg and a simple virus.

▶ A Father Feels His Son's Pain

The *Chovos HaLevavos* explains that a father feels his son's pain like his own. A father views his son as an extension of himself. So, it's not his son's arm that's being cut, it's his own.

We recognize this as paternal instinct. But where does that instinct come from? Why do parents feel such a powerful connection to their children? Why would a parent be willing to give up their life for a child?

Hashem wants children to be loved and cared for, so He created this instinct, and implanted into the heart of man a sense of devotion to their offspring.

In plain language, any mercy that a child experiences came about because Hashem created those sentiments. When I was a young boy and stepped on a nail, I went running to my mother. The reason she gathered me in her arms and comforted me, was because Hashem wanted me to feel secure. Once I cut my arm and cried out in horror, "All of my blood is spilling out!" My father scooped me up and calmed me down, because Hashem wanted me to be cared for. Any kindness or love that I have ever experienced was created by Hashem.

LIFE LESSON

Hashem loves you, more than you love you!

Chapter Twenty-One
Stop Playing God

Eighty percent of our *emunah* problems and ninety percent of our questions on HASHEM stem from one mistake—we play God. Playing God means I know exactly what I need. I need to marry *that* woman. I need *that* job. I need my child to get into *that* school.

I've talked to HASHEM about it. I've explained it to Him. I've even brokered deals with Him. "If You grant me this, I'll…"

Yet for some reason, He just won't listen.

"HASHEM, what's the deal? Are You angry with me? Are You punishing me? Why do You insist on making my life so difficult? This is what I need. Why won't You just listen to me?"

And I go on asking questions. "It's not fair. It doesn't make sense! HASHEM, what do You want from me?"

The problem here is quite simple—I am playing God. And I'm not God. The simple reality is that *maybe*, just *maybe*, it's not going because it's not *supposed* to go. Maybe HASHEM knows better than I do what is for my best. "Hmmmm... I never thought about that..."

▶ Historical Perspective

This is peculiar because I've lived through situations that didn't turn out as I thought they would. I absolutely had to have *that* job; it was just what I needed. I could earn a living, support my family, and still have time to learn. It was the perfect fit. In the end, I didn't get the job, and I had major questions. "HASHEM, why?! Why aren't You there for me?" Then, five years later, I find out that the entire industry is being shipped over to India. Oh...

A different time, I tried to marry that woman. She was perfect; great match, good family. She would make a fantastic wife and mother for my children. And it didn't go. "HASHEM, why have you abandoned me? This is what I need!" She ended up marrying someone else. Then, two years later, I find out that the term "mentally unstable" is a mild description of her situation. Mmmmm…

Then it was my son. My son absolutely, positively, had to get into that class; it was just what he needed. Great *rebbe*, good atmosphere—it was perfect. And the *menahel* wouldn't let. "HASHEM, why? Where are You?" Then, two months later, I found out that there's a child in that class who would have been the worst possible influence on my son. It would have been devastating. Hmmmm…

▶ Part Of Human Nature

The ironic part is that we do this all the time. We act as if we truly know what is best for us. We run after it. We hotly pursue it.

"No obstacle will stand in *my* way. Nothing will prevent *this* from coming about."

And when lo and behold, my efforts are thwarted—the questions begin. "But, why? It's not fair! I am a good person. HASHEM, why won't You just help me?"

It's easy to see the folly of this when other people do it, but when it happens in my world, then the real challenge begins. To break out of this, we need to change perspective.

▶ Hashem Knows Better Than I Do What Is For My Best

The concept we need to embrace is that *Hashem knows better than I do what is best for me*. As smart as I may be, and as clear as it is to me that this is what I need, Hashem still knows better. That is the second condition of *bitachon*.

In theory, this should be easy to see. After all, how much do I know? How far into the future can I really see? But the problem isn't in the world of theory. The problem is in my world—in the thick and thin of life.

It's when I know so clearly that this is what I need and it's not happening that the challenge begins.

So I go back and forth in my mind. "Yes, I would like to trust Hashem, but… how can I possibly believe that Hashem is doing this for my good? I *know* it's not true. You can't ask me to accept something I know is false. If I weren't sure, it would be one thing, but this is so clear and so obvious. I know what I need."

▶ The Solution: The Bigger Picture

The solution is to put some perspective into my thinking.

Often it requires talking to myself, having actual conversations in my mind where I challenge myself.

"Let's see… Who should I trust—myself or Hashem? Well, let's do the math. Who am I? Who is Hashem?

"Hashem created the heavens and the earth and all that they contain. He wrote the formulas for quantum physics and molecular biology. He views the entire universe with one glance. He sees the future as the past. And He has the wisdom to see far-reaching results. What will this bring to ten years from now? What will the consequences be twenty years from now?

"I, on the other hand, see about two inches in front of my face. I make mistakes. I get confused and caught up. I forget. I forget lessons. I forget facts. I forget consequences. I can't remember what I had for breakfast this morning. And as much as I think I know, I am often wrong. That which I think will be so good for me, so many times isn't.

"Hashem, on the other hand, remembers every event since Creation. Hashem sees from one end of history to the other. And Hashem made me. He is my Creator, and *He knows me even better than I do, so He understands my needs better than I do.*

"Who do I think has it right? Me or Hashem? Me or Hashem? Mmmmm. Let me get back to you on that one."

LIFE LESSON

Hashem knows better than you do what is for your best.

Chapter Twenty-Two
No Regrets

While I was a young man learning in *kollel*, I found out that Amazon.com was going public. I had been a fan of Amazon for many years, and I was intrigued by their business model. Every order was delivered on time, every time – exactly as promised. It seemed to be a company poised for success.

Still, my wife and I were newly married and money wasn't plentiful, so when I discussed the idea with her, she was a bit hesitant, but said, "If you feel it's a good idea, go ahead." So we agreed that the next day I would invest two thousand dollars in the initial public offering.

That night, for some reason, my wife turned to the business section of Newsweek and read an article about Amazon. "Jeff Bezos has a million dollars in personal credit card debt...He is asking fifteen dollars a share...The company has nowhere near that market value..." On and on, the article ragged against the stock.

My wife brought the piece to me. "What do you want to do?" she asked.

"What do *you* want to do?" I responded.

"I think it's just too risky."

"OK, fine."

And I didn't purchase the stock.

Let's imagine for a moment that I had. And let's say that I had held onto those shares till today. The last time I counted, those two thousand dollars were worth 1.4 million dollars. 1.4 million dollars is a tidy sum of money! Not that we lack, but I can think of some clever things to do with 1.4 million dollars. *Aw, shucks!*

Aw, shucks is a lack of *bitachon*. *Aw, shucks* means, "If only I would have convinced her. Why didn't I push harder? I could have, should have, would have …"

However, if I accept that every Rosh Hashanah HASHEM decrees how much money I will make that year – that means that I accept that HASHEM decrees how much money I will make that year. A lot or a little. A huge fortune or whatever. But that is the point. HASHEM is in charge. He runs the world. He knows what is best for me and He orchestrates events the way He sees is for the best.

And so, for some *strange reason*, my wife just happened to read that section of Newsweek the very night before I was to buy those shares. Even though she doesn't normally read the business section. And even though Time magazine had a very different take on the situation, and had she read *that* article, she would have had a different opinion. But she read the Newsweek article at that time, and brought it to my attention because that money wasn't supposed to be part of our future.

This is a critical factor in learning to trust HASHEM. Whether I recognize it as good or not, I trust that HASHEM knows better than I, and HASHEM orchestrates the events of my life for my good.

In this case, it doesn't take a rocket scientist to recognize why a young fellow in *kollel* might be better off without 1.4 million dollars. But that is the point. One who trusts in HASHEM has no regrets. No *could have, should have, would have*. "Oh, I should have invested in real estate in the eighties!" "Why didn't I buy gold when it was up!?" "Why didn't I get out of the market a year earlier?" All of these are the words of a person who is in this world on his own – a man who enters the uncertainty of a volatile marketplace, alone. And then he suffers regrets. Regret that he didn't buy more. Regret that he didn't get that lucky break. Regret that he chose what he chose.

If I wasn't sensible or if I didn't do my due diligence, then there is plenty of room for regret. But that regret is because *I* failed. *I* wasn't wise. *I* didn't act as I should have. But assuming that I was judicious and prudent, then I have full trust in Hashem. Hashem directs every transaction. Hashem knows better than I what is for my best, and Hashem orchestrates events towards that end. And therefore, there is no remorse, no regret.

Hashem knows better than I do what is best for me.

LIFE LESSON

**Regret stems from not accepting that HASHEM controls all outcomes.
A person with perfect Bitachon, will never experience regret.**

Chapter Twenty-Three
Why Is Life So Difficult?

Financial worries, health issues, trouble with children, in law problems, marital conflicts...the list seem endless. One of the questions a thinking person should ask is why? Why is life so hard? Why are there so many issues, worries and anxieties that afflict man? And worse it doesn't stop. Just when things are starting to move smoothly, something else pops up—and undoes it all. It almost seems orchestrated. The perplexing part is that we aren't talking about wicked individuals. We're talking about good people. People who do what they should be doing—and yet they suffer in very real ways. The question we need to ask is why?

We accept that HASHEM is more giving and loving than any person we could ever imagine or envision. And HASHEM is very capable. HASHEM could have easily made man very differently. HASHEM could have made life very differently, and there wouldn't be any suffering. Not a little, not a lot—none. And so the question that begs being asked is why. Why is life so difficult? Why does it seem to be so hard?

To understand this we need a different perspective of life.

▶ Progressive Weight Training

A rather yeshivishe fellow went to a power-lifting gym to learn how to work out. As a kid, he had little experience with sports and was clearly out of his element. Recognizing this, the coach showed him various exercises and worked closely with him.

One day this fellow was overheard saying, *"That coach, I don't know what's with him. Every time I get the exercise right, he goes and adds more weight to the bar. What's wrong with him?"*

The point this fellow missed was that **progressive weight training** is all about increasing the load. The goal of the activity is to coax the body to grow. By gradually increasing the work load, the body is called upon to respond. The work should never be easy. The nature of the activity is to incrementally increase the demand placed on the body, thereby causing it to grow.

This is a good parable because in life we are put into many situations. If a person doesn't understand why he is on this planet, he will have many questions. Why does it seem that there is a never ending stream of difficult situations? Why is it that when I finally get things under control, a whole new set of circumstances arises that sets everything out of kilter? Why can't life just be easy?

The point that he is missing is the very purpose of life. Hashem put us on this planet to grow. Many of the challenges and situations are given to us specifically for that reason. It isn't by accident, and it isn't because Hashem doesn't pay attention. Quite the opposite, these situations were hand-designed to demand from us. They are catalysts to change who we are.

In weight training, the movement of the bar isn't the significant part; the demand on the body is. So too in life, the situations I face are far less significant than my reactions to them. Who I become is a result of my attitude and the way I handle my challenges.

The end result is that life is beautiful, but it isn't a walk in the park. A life properly led will have moments of doubt, pain, and confusion. That doesn't mean that we are on the wrong path, and it doesn't mean that life doesn't make sense. Quite the opposite, if life is going too smoothly, it's a bad sign. Since the purpose of life is to grow, we need the challenges of life to help us reach our potential.

LIFE LESSON

In weight training, the movement of the bar isn't significant; the demand on the body is. In life, the situations I face are far less significant than my reactions to them. Who I become is a result of my attitude and the way I handle my challenges.

Chapter Twenty-Four
Virtual Boxing Game

If you enter a video arcade, you might notice the boxing game. For your two dollars in tokens, you get to fight a *virtual* professional boxer. When you put your money in and put the gloves on, up on the screen the referee will appear to usher you and your opponent into the center of the ring. And then, " Ding!" — the action starts. Jab, jab, duck, punch. Jab, jab, duck, punch. Your opponent circles. He swings wide, you block and counter. THUD! He falls to the canvas. The count: 1, 2, 3. . . But no. He's back up and now on the offensive. He throws a power right to your midsection — thud! Now, a hook to your jaw — smash! Now it's you that's down. The count 1, 2, 3, 4. . . but you're back up, and the fight continues. Jab, jab, hook. Duck. Jab, jab. Move right. The bell rings again, signaling the end of the round.

And you are sweating. No matter what shape you are in, the pace is so fast and the simulation so real that you are putting everything into it. And then you go to spend the rest of your day with your children. No headaches, no bruises.

If you speak to someone who has been in a real boxing ring, you get a very different picture. Likely, you will hear something like, "Nothing in my life prepared me for those two minutes — the punches to the jaw, the jabs to the head, and more than anything, the fear that at any moment this beast is going to smash my brains in. . ." All of that make boxing a very different experience than the boxing arcade. It's a whole lot less fun.

▶ Life Is Like A Video Game

This is a very apt parable for life. Throughout our lives, HASHEM puts us through many different situations, all measured, all finely focused for our growth. Some are tests of endurance, some are tests of faith, and some are tests of patience, but each one is custom-designed for our growth.

But like a video game — it's not real. It's a mirage, just a frightening image. When it is over, we see it for what it was — an empty threat.

The *Chovos HaLevovos* (*Shaar HaBitachon*) explains that one of the basics of our belief system is, –"You can't harm me; you can't help me." Everything is decreed by HASHEM. Every ounce of suffering, every event that is to befall a person, is all decided, defined and directed by HASHEM Himself. No human being can inflict damage to me that wasn't already decided by HASHEM.

With this cognition comes a deep understanding: the doctor isn't the determinant of whether I live or die; the threat isn't the failing economy; the danger isn't man. All humans are powerless to affect my destiny. Like a simulated opponent in an arcade game, they look very menacing, but it is just smoke and mirrors. HASHEM is hiding behind every scene, orchestrating the outcome. And all along, I am always safe and sound, guarded and protected.

The various life challenges that we are presented with are a significant tool in our development. As we face them, if we feel a sense of dread and anxiety, it is time for us to ask ourselves: Who runs the world? The more that we come to understand that HASHEM is always present, controlling every situation, the more we feel a sense of calm security. Ultimately, our job is to be able to see the threats for what they are: mere bluffs — changing video games to challenge us to grow.

LIFE LESSON

HASHEM creates many custom made situations, all designed for our growth.

Chapter Twenty-Five
What Real Bitachon Feels Like

Imagine a five-year-old, walking with her mother into the hospital for her second chemotherapy treatment. The little girl knows what's coming. She remembers the pain. She understands the nausea. She knows what it's like to brush her hair and watch clumps come out. Yet, she holds her mother's hand, and goes along, because "Mommy said I need to do this."

The child doesn't understand cancer. She certainly doesn't understand how throwing up for a week cures it. But she knows that Mommy loves her. She knows that Mommy takes care of her. And she knows that Mommy knows what's best.

She fully trusts her mother.

That is the type of trust we can develop in Hashem—the almost blind trust of the child. I know that Hashem is looking out for my best interests. I know that Hashem loves me more than I love myself. And I know that Hashem knows better than I do what's for my best. So I trust Hashem. I trust that Hashem is right here, in charge of my life, orchestrating the events for my ultimate good.

So I walk through life fully confident. Not confident that things will turn out as I have planned them. Not confident that life will have a Hollywood ending. But confident that Hashem has chosen the best path for me, and is leading me down it. So I take Hashem's hand, so to speak, and walk with unwavering trust.

▶ Taking Control of My Thoughts

One of the best techniques to grow in trusting Hashem is to memorize certain phrases and repeat them over and over like a mantra: *Hashem loves me more than I love myself. Hashem knows better than I do what is for my best.*

When I say these phrases again and again, they start to sink in. I begin to recognize on an *emotional level* that "I don't really know." I learn to trust in HASHEM's wisdom and kindness. And then I can do that which we humans find so difficult to do—accept what HASHEM has decreed with joy.

LIFE LESSON

To grow in bitachon certain phrases must become habitual.
Two such phrases are:
1. Hashem loves me more than I love myself.
2. Hashem knows better than I do what is for my best.

Where Do We Go From Here

I hope that you have found this book meaningful. While it offers information, its primary purpose is to impart a perspective – a perspective that should be the underpinnings of everything that we do.

The question is: where do we go from here? What is the next step?

A tool that I would like to suggest is *"The Shmuz."* The Shmuz is exactly what the title implies, a mussar (ethics) "talk" that deals with a wide range of subjects: davening, emunah, bitachon, marriage, parenting, people skills, working on anger, jealousy and humility.... At this point, there are over two hundred lectures, and the list is growing. Similar in style to the book that you have just read, the Shmuz takes the Torah sources and applies it to life – to your life in the twenty first century.

The lectures are available in a number of portals, and one is the Shmuz.com. There you can listen, watch, read, download or podcast.

If you are from an earlier age, or if you try to avoid internet usage, there are still a number of ways to access the Shmuz. There are CDs of the audio, books on various topics, and you can listen to the Shmuz on Kol Halashon.

If you would like more information, or would like to bring the Shmuz to your community, please call the Shmuz office at 1- 866-613-TORAH (8672). Or by e- mail Binny@theshmuz.com.

Made in the USA
Columbia, SC
18 January 2023